PRAISE FOR RHIA!

Rhian Elizabeth's poetry reminds us that the
and sometimes plain old fun. Read these poe
reckoning, the yes yes yes to life.
— Joseph Fasano

There is an ease to these poems which makes them feel like 'memorable
speech' - they slip straight from the page as though spoken out loud.
— Andrew McMillan

girls etc sings with heartbreak, dating rituals, love, loss and a Garden of Eden
rewrite. This collection is a good friend — sometimes painfully honest, but
mostly makes you feel "apple crumble warm".
— Hanan Issa, National Poet of Wales

three days after she broke my nose / we pinned up bunting'. *girls etc* is an
important book which confronts frankly experiences of abuse in a lesbian
relationship. The tender poems here unpacking motherhood and queer
love are made all the more poignant through this contrast. Elsewhere,
imaginative flourishes sparkle in the dark: a lover expands like an accordion,
planting bulbs becomes 'an octopus funeral' and someone whose life is a
Netflix series hangs around in 'the empty silver static'. This is passionate,
resonant writing.
— John McCullough

in *girls etc* love is a messy business whose backdrop is the sound of hard and
honest rain. In *girls etc* i found heartbreak with Bette Davis, Keira Knightley,
Taylor Swift and Agnetha from Abba. Here a young mother breaks gently
through patchouli scented flats, chewing gum covered welsh pavements
and out into startling Swedish nights. In this gritty, witty, and often delicate
collection of poems I found "naked and holy places" tucked between such
fleeting moments of love.
— Jessica Mookherjee

Also by Rhian Elizabeth

Six Pounds Eight Ounces   (Seren Books, 2014)

the last polar bear on earth   (Parthian Books, 2018)

GIRLS ETC

Rhian Elizabeth was born in 1988 in the Rhondda Valley, South Wales. She is a Hay Festival Writer at Work and Writer in Residence at the Coracle International Literary Festival in Tranås, Sweden. She is currently at night school studying to be a counsellor.

ISBN: 978-1-915760-62-3

Cover designed by Aaron Kent

Edited and Typeset by Aaron Kent

Broken Sleep Books Ltd
PO BOX 102
Llandysul
SA44 9BG

Contents

for Scout

girls etc

Rhian Elizabeth

Broken Sleep Books

september 30th, 2005

this is how it starts for us,
the both of us screaming,
your little lungs giving out their very first roar
and me, on the other end of the cord,
left smouldering in the embers
of that temporary madness...

         and now, all these years later,
         that cord has been cut,
         you still have the lungs of a lion,
         and we are both still screaming.

the daughters of eden

think of that garden.
the rivers, the flowers
and the trees. how god mixed
it on his palette – the very first
shade of the colour green – and then,
like monet, slung it from his paintbrush
at the earth's blank canvas. *paradise.* not one
pristine blade of grass yet trampled by the careless foot of man.

we know what happened next

but what if god didn't create adam?
what if, instead, he first made eve and then plucked
from her rib *another* eve?   no cain and abel to follow
because he knew it, even then, that women make terrible mothers.

would either eve have snatched
the forbidden apple from the tree,
given in to temptation?

i would have been too preoccupied with her nakedness
to even notice the serpent.

midsummer

the potatoes are cut in half
the meatballs are fried
the salad is washed and tossed
slices of salmon are lifted out
of a vacuum pack with a knife
then delicately laid across
a handsome china plate
a wedge of lemon is placed in the middle
like a yellow island floating
on a pastel pink sea
there's pickled herring
herbs or chives
or something
and chunky soured cream
the wine pours and pours
like the rain outside the window
and we've been downing schnapps
since well before 10am
deadly shots of vodka with a thump of cumin
fennel or aniseed
or something
this will be my fourth one and this is *not*
going to end well i know
but hey!
i'm in sweden

it's tradition
and who am *i* to fly in and question
tradition.

it starts like this

you meet on the internet.
up until now you've thought
this sort of thing beneath you;
online dating is something
only desperate people do.

how fucking tragic to put yourself
on display like that, like a nearly
out of date packet of ham all sad
and sweating up on the reduced
shelf in the fridge of romance.

oh love me, *PLEASE*!

but against your better judgment

here
you
are
swiping
and
there
she
is

smiling.

the show off

the others do not notice (the rest of
your group are standing with hands on
hips, nervously peering over the edge
and weighing up the drop into the water)
that you have already taken your clothes off,
shed them like a snakeskin.

they are debating the laws of science (the chances
of impaling oneself on the jutting stones that jab at the
air below like medieval silver swords) as you launch
yourself off the fifty-foot high rockface the locals
here in tranås call *troll's rock,*
shrieking in gleeful triumph.

the landing is where your bravado ends.

you are a fucking idiot (and perhaps you always knew it,
but you are definitely sure of it now, new-born naked,
thrashing about like a startled foetus trying to find the exit
door of its mother's womb), the water is unforgivingly freezing,
and you've massively misjudged your swimming abilities -
you're lucky to reach the surface alive.

but despite this initial encounter, to that lake
you return and return, make the daily walk

through the neighbourhood of charming,
oh so swedish houses to get there, past the
manicured lawns and lollypop stick fences,
like a pilgrim on a journey to the holy place.

that lake *is* your holy place.

the silence there is a sacrifice, the long wooden jetty is an alter,
each skimming of the lake's surface by a kaleidoscope-coloured
dragonfly is a whispered, humming prayer that only *you* can hear.
if john the baptist was around you'd ask him to gently lower you in,
anoint your sweaty brow, and get him to explain it, the deal with water...
what it is that makes it so mending.

that lake seems to forgive you. for everything.

keira knightley

you don't know why you're remembering this now,
after all these years, but your whole body winces
in horror when the memory randomly comes

to you like an unsolicited takeaway menu through the letterbox.
what on earth were you thinking? what kind of fucking madness was
going on in your knickers that could've ever possessed you to do it?

what you did:

you tried to recreate the scene from love actually. the one where a hopeless
loser, all doe-eyed and despairing, tries to win keira knightley over with a
series of cards on which he's written declarations of his unrequited love.

what you didn't think of:

that, unlike in the film, this theatrical spectacle of yours was not set on
a picture-perfect, snow-dusted, chrstimassy-warm street somewhere in
swanky london. nope it was a grim july in the south wales valleys, outside
a stinking,

pissy pub in your old university town. pavement covered in chewing gum
and dog shit. the sky threatening- then delivering on cue- rain. and there
you were standing in the drizzle, holding up these soggy cards in front of
this speechless girl.

why you did it?

fuck knows now. but you did things like that when you were younger.
things you thought made you interesting, things you thought could
compensate for the things you could *not* do, like trust. you offered gestures
in place of feelings. you played games you thought you could win

when all you really should've done
was be yourself.

girls don't hurt girls

what was it that bette davis
said about joan crawford?
that she had slept with every
male star at mgm except lassie

and then joan crawford said that
bette davis lacked the absence of any real
beauty and girls will be girls when
there are boys involved and egos at stake

but this wasn't like that   she hurt me

why didn't you tell the police?

i almost did   a few times

but then i'd remember break time
in the yard at primary school,
and janie with her spite and her
names and her chinese burns

i did the right thing then   i told the teacher

just to be sent back to the yard,
arm glowing red, with instructions

to forget all about it and play nice,
knowing that if that was rhys or daniel
and they had singled me out and booted
a football at me on purpose or something
they would've been sent straight
to the headmistress's office

so that was that, retreating to the silent corner of
the yard, my tears and my throbbing arm, the faint
chalk markings of an old hopscotch ladder on the ground,
and smug janie walking by smiling a horrible smile

tell on me again and next time i will do it harder

mother & daughter ripping

when we fight i storm off into the meadow of buttercups
        behind our house like i am a great gust
            of wind sweeping through it

rip them out of the ground like a lion ripping flesh off a
        meaty bone & they don't deserve it, the buttercups,
            minding their own business

i am ripping petals & turning them into
        pieces of golden confetti, throwing them into
            the mercy of the breeze

all the while she is ripping clothes out of drawers
        & ripping posters off walls i could rip
            this damn meadow clean of buttercups

& when i'm done with the slaughter i go home
        her clothes are everywhere i am sweating & covered in dirt
            & neither of us says a word until she asks me

what's for tea?

i am the captain

in films and tv shows
they always give boats female names
so i name this one after
the best lover
i ever had
it is rude to say
now i can ride her!
i never did learn
how to properly handle a vessel
as mighty as a woman
i turn the key in the ignition
the open ocean beckons
her engine rumbles
and i am the captain.

dear harriet

knowing something of suffering, i always
think of you here at sommen. the same lake
you saw through your window, all those
years cooped up in the romanäs sanatorium

slowly coughing out your corroding lungs-
tuberculosis, the souvenir you brought back
with you from ceylon. but since, like me,
you always searched for the humour in

your darkness, i know you will not mind it
when i say: you sure had a view to die for!
looking out at all this blue, alone and frail
and fading, you wrote of your plight:

nu har till sist jag blitt så sur och lessen –

now i'm so sad and sour.

oh darling,
me too!

Harriet Löwenhjelm
Poet and Painter
1887 – 1918

the wheatsheaf, fitzrovia, london

rumour has it that when augustus john nipped to the loo
for a piss that is the moment dylan thomas swooped

in on caitlin, drunk as a skunk in the dark
and smoky salon, thus sealing caitlin's fate to be

immortalised in ink instead of paint. and it is in
this very pub you turn my knuckles rollercoaster

white under the table, wary of any roaming dylan thomas',
not because you are scared of poets, but you whisper

that i am a slut. and so here it is, babe
your cruelty, immortalised in *my* ink.

death of a sunflower

i meant it when i said
you are special.

and, like the sunflowers
that continue and continue
to grow on the tuscan fields,
summer after summer,
august after august,
you *too* will continue.

each sunflower's life ends, of course,
as everything that begins must end

but not yet

not *yet.*

can't we just watch
the rising of thousands
of yellow miracles out
from the darkness below,
without asking questions?

love without tongues

i only survived my school days
because of you. two class clowns
who were never in class, our ties
drooping like dead snakes around
our necks, missing lesson after lesson,
certain in our conviction that listening
to nirvana's nevermind on repeat in
your bedroom beneath cigarette smoke
clouds was much more important

(which it was)

remember
how the other girls wouldn't even sit
by us in the changing room
because we were *lesbians?*

we fancied a lot of girls

girls	with braces
girls	with violin cases
girls	with skirts
	so short
	they left nothing to our imaginations
girls	who stuffed balls of kleenex down their bras

girls   who didn't need to
girls   with bubblegum globes inflating
          like strawberry scented planets between their lips
          those mouthy girls who sold single cigs
          round the back of the english block for
          an extortionate pound, though we would've
          happily given them all the change in the
          front pockets of our rucksacks

          (if they'd asked for it)

dating girls and comparing their scores
like we were playing top trumps

our hearts got broken more times
than the ringer on the school bell

but it wasn't ever like *that*
between the two of us
we never even talked much
about anything

not about how i felt when my father died,
or if you were scared when you watched yours
knocking your mother around. i never even asked
you why you cut up the skin on your arms but then
again you didn't bat an eyelid when i got pregnant at 16

that was just the way it was, i guess.

ours was love without tongues   in more ways than one.

it's good to see you

dying was easy   not like living

our lives were a netflix series
made for fans of the repetitively tragic and macabre
     the two of us the main characters
and neither one of us deserved what they put us through
     season after season

and when i got cancelled i told every lover
who came after you that they were the best
     the incantation left my lips each time
like a prayer from a sinner on death row
     the last false words to god in the hope
of altering favourably what comes next

but dying was   not like living

it was falling asleep under blankets warmed on the radiator
a belly full of favourite snacks
     the two cats purring at the foot of the bed
the tv screen a night light in the dark
     and the credits rolling on and on and on

i just stayed there in the afterlife
hung around the empty silver static
      rehearsing the lines i would say to you
when you finally made it over

i've waited a long time

it's good to see you.

patchouli

on nights i'd go to see her she'd leave the key to her apartment
for me underneath the green wheelie bin on the gravel out front.
i'd busy myself until she got back, mostly by browsing her dvd
shelf and giving myself a little tour of the place, stroking her many
cats (she had 5). i had no clue about what she'd been doing or where
she'd been, she'd just go around filling the cat bowls with biscuits
and water, and then we'd get down to the business of what i was there
for- watching dvds and fucking. she'd light incense sticks to cover
up the cat shit smell. i can still taste that awful combination in my
mouth now- patchouli and shit- and that was that until the next time i
came over and rummaged around the gravel in the dark for the feel of keys.
i broke it off when i found out what she did for a living, not that i judged
her for it or because i was in any way disgusted, but it's just that when you
grow up as an only child, you are not cut out for sharing your things.

my daughter eats a roast dinner on skype

she is an artist

i watch her
decorate
each item
on her plate

                          with mint sauce
                          that drips
                          like green paint
                          off her spoon

                                                reluctantly she eats
                                                her way through
                                                the vegetables
                                                saving her favourites

(the roast potatoes
and the yorkshire
puddings)
until last

                          we never want
                          the things
                          we love
                          the most

                          to end

the vulture

in spite of our very worst efforts
we don't make each other happy

still i circle you
like a starving bird scavenging

the same old bones.

new pathways

you don't know how you ended up in a place like this
like *this*. leaflets spread out across the console table.
a fake plant in the corner of the hallway. the cd player
playing the exact same gentle tune each time you take
a seat in the waiting area.

you can see that she's been crying, but you don't speak
to the sad girl sitting next to you. you never speak to any
of the sad girls sitting next to you.

you are not silenced anymore but still, here you all are,
just staring at the once pretty and ornate chipped green
titles on the floor. the colour must've faded a long time ago –
worn down by all the footprints, of all the once broken girls.

the flea market of feelings

the guitar she claims she can play but won't
is collecting its daily downpour of dust
the boxes of magazines and books are bending
towards the ceiling like a lost city of leaning towers of pisa
the trinkets and ornaments are leaking from supermarket
carrier bags like brass and gold and china innards
the christmas tree that stays up all year round is naked and sad
the plants on the windowsill have given up on living
the knives and forks and spoons are caked in gunk
the plates and bowls and mugs are half full of various floating things
orange peel curls, soggy cereal hoops
the half burned yankee candle jars are scentless
the phone chargers and tv remotes may or may not be broken
the empty photo frames on the mantelpiece
are tiny windows without a view
the black sacks bulging with letters to and from old lovers
look like tombstones

all these weapons at her disposal, objects that fly
like bats around this graveyard of memories

there is a smell in here that i won't forget
like damp and dog and rotting
like sex i am forced to have

yet i don't fight back
        like a coward

i just hoard my feelings

the way she hoards her things.

rökstenen

when his son vämod died
varin carved his memories into this giant stone
that has stood in the churchyard for a thousand years
stoic through the polar nights
snow-capped under the aurora borealis
but red hot to the touch this afternoon

this scorched & parched summer
is one of the driest in sweden
since records began...

go on and press your ear against the runes, you tell me

listen

listen closely for the sound of rain.

Rökstenen is one of Sweden's most famous runestones. Its inscription, with its 760 characters, is considered the longest runic inscription in the world. The smokestone is sometimes said to be the starting point for the history of Swedish literature as the oldest surviving literary work.

monster

three days after she broke my nose
we pinned up bunting, black triangles
with skeletons on, carved faces into human
head-sized pumpkins, made mozzarella ghosts
as toppings for our homemade pizza...

throughout the night kids came by exuberantly flipping
the letterbox; a conveyer belt of witches, vampires
and monsters chanting trick or treat in the moonlight.
the colour around my eyes a mixture of purple
and yellow and green, the bridge of my nose bent
into a shape not too dissimilar to one of the little witches'...

she dropped lollipops and miniature packets of haribo
into the kids' plastic buckets that were overflowing
with bright bright candy. she feigned horror and told them
that they were very scary indeed as they moved on to
the neighbour's house, pounding their letterbox,
blissfully unaware that the real monster
was this side of the door.

taylor. fucking. swift.

thanks to my teenage daughter, if you dare me to sing you
every single song taylor swift has ever written, i could easily
do it, lyric perfect too. in our house taylor's name is sacred,
her face repeated on our walls like the image of our blessed

lady mary, and i feel i ought to make the sign of the cross each
time i pass it, even though i am not a practising catholic. i once
asked my daughter who she would save if we were both drowning,
me or taylor (she could only choose one of us), and i knew

by the awkward silence that followed that it would be me left sinking,
mouth open in a silent scream, while taylor is pulled from the water,
caramel hair falling in perfect, wet curls like an all-american mermaid,
ready to write her next song about heartbreak.

agnetha fältskog

he must've passed that sign for jönköping, your hometown, too, when he drove all the way from holland/ one thousand miles in the snow/ just to tell you that he had loved you since he was eight years old/ now a man with a dangerous infatuation/ he ransacked every town in sweden until he found you/ no longer the smiling bombshell in the shimmering sequin suit, your ice blue eyes were sad as your tried to put the pieces of your life back together/ the breakdown of your marriages, the suicide of your mother and the death of your father had left you broken/ and when he said *he'd* never leave you, i guess that was appealing/ but now like icarus after he flew too close to the sun, that little boy staring at the superstar taped to his ceiling sits bald and fat and alone in his forklift truck/ with a restraining order/ still writing you letter after unanswered letter.

fixing

there is overgrown ivy in my chest
a heap of unkempt nettles and leaves

a sharp, green nest of nasty things
that i ought to take the sheers to

but instead i evict reluctant weeds
from the gaps in the patio stones

paint the rotting fence a rose petal pink
let the mower loose on the feral grass

i preside over an octopus funeral
burying bulbs that look like sea creatures

hang bamboo chimes and curling wind turners
from the branches of the stately ash tree

that, like a tattered canopy, casts a broken shadow
over the dahlias in terra cotta pots

i watch with motherly pride a round bellied finch
peck seeds off the feeding table i built

i've worked so hard fixing this mad old garden
but i don't know how to start the work

of fixing myself.

packing grief into boxes

the night our cat died it snowed while we slept, our bodies froze together in the bed as if we were solidified by the sadness. we woke to all the cars on our street blanketed in white, the blizzard had transformed them into statues that no shovel would be able to dig out for days. then i spotted them across the roof of our ford fiesta, this trail of little paw prints stamped into the snow.

i never told her this, but when she was busy with something around the house, i put my wellies on and went into the garden. there were branches dripping with ice, flowers twinkling like they were made of glass, like hidden treasure revealing itself. and there it was, that awful little mountain, my makeshift cross of twigs at the summit barely standing upright with the weight of snow.

i don't know what i was thinking. of course it was still there. i had lay him in that shoebox and buried him myself.

we broke up a few years later, gave up the rental on the house, packed our things into boxes and argued over who was going to get the aquarium,

whose fault it all was. and i know that we left
him behind in the garden there, but every time it
falls, i still look for paw prints in the snow.

i always ordered the lobster fra diavolo

all date night achieved was reaffirming
the fact that we were no longer the same people.
the red tiffany lamp hanging over the darkened
booth still pushed crimson triangles of light across
the tablecloth, you wore the black dress you thought
was my favourite, and when he came to take our order,
the owner of the restaurant said he was glad to see us again-
his favourite customers, why had we not a-come back
to see him for so long?
we made our excuses, reinvented the story of our lives,
and you hesitated about your selection.
but i knew exactly what i wanted.
i was always so predictable, and you said that was the problem.
stomach rumbling, my heart sank when i saw it, the marker pen
through the belly of the words;

they'd taken the lobster fra diavolo off the menu.

squeezebox

i loved you   i think   if love is like   stretching a person out
like an accordion   seeing all their folds   and never wanting
the   music   to   stop.

if we could just go back i'd push you higher

at the playground the stink from last night's fire on the
mountain infiltrates the summer air, lingering like bad breath

you send the pushchair toppling, come flying out of the seat
as soon as i release the clip like you're a parachuter ejecting

i sit on a bench and watch you zoom around,
free falling between the various apparatus

up the steps and down the slide   up the steps and down the slide

swinging from the bars
like a curly yellow haired little monkey

you ride the seesaw solo
adamant that it's a unicorn

up the steps and down the slide   up the steps and down the slide

until you summon me over to the swings
where i push you half-heartedly

chubby toes wriggling in your sandals
clumps of pink varnish spread haphazardly across the nails

as if you've been colouring outside the lines
but you insisted on doing it all by yourself

or maybe i was too busy?

this poem is a memory

19 years old and playing at being a mother
the way you played with your dolls

you deserved so much better, *so* much better
and now it spins and it spins and it spins

guilt   is a roundabout
                 that won't ever let you get off.

cease fire

the day will come when our hair is white
two tangled puffs of clouds
rising from our armchairs
the clock ticking like a time bomb
on the living room wall
the sound of pomegranates being pried apart

all our nights like this, apple crumble warm

we'll encourage the cats to finish their dinners
the things that happened such a long time ago
just cobwebs left to inhabit the corner of the ceiling
we will forget the names of our favourite songs
and my sides will be bruised with laughter.

lesbians r us

i had a girlfriend who was so beautiful it was terrifying

i was like a kid emerging from the toy store

carrying an expensive china doll that i knew

my behaviour hadn't been anywhere near good enough to deserve

 that if i had saved up my pocket money for ten years

i still wouldn't have been able to afford her

but somehow i had her

and i was so afraid i would drop her

that she would fall to the pavement

smash into pieces.

*it takes a woman on average 7 attempts
to leave an abusive relationship*

like the dirty city at sunset
when the awesome light sinks
behind the grey tower blocks
you could be pretty in moments

and that is why
i stayed.

outer space, out of time

when you were a baby
you wouldn't sleep unless it was next to me

> you screamed our little house down
> the second i lay you in your cot

i tried rocking you back and forth
singing every nursery rhyme known to man

> but no lullaby could ever persuade you
> to settle into a dream

the solar system mobile would still be
playing twinkle twinkle little star

> as i gave in, carried you resentfully to my bed
> and you would be *smiling* then, silent as a stone

during those never-ending nights
milk circles spilling wet planets onto the sheets

> i thought it was a curse
> but eighteen years later you flinch at my touch

you want to cast a galaxy between us
> and now i understand that it was all a blessing.

Acknowledgements

Broken Sleep Books and Aaron Kent.

Zoë Brigley and *Poetry Wales* for publishing previous editions of some of these poems.

Clare Potter, Rebecca Parfitt, Catrin Kean, Louise Walsh, Fizzy Oppe, Susie Wildsmith, Tiffany Murray and Mark Blayney.

Tack så mycket Eleanor Shaw, Dominic Williams and the rest of my Swedish family in Tranås and beyond — for making me feel so welcome in Sweden and providing a sanctuary for me there when I needed it the most. Thanks for all the swims in Vättern and Sommen and Trollsjön.

And thanks always to Scout, who I am endlessly proud of.

Galop is the UK'S LGBT+ anti-abuse charity. They work with and for LGBT+ victims and survivors of interpersonal abuse and violence **www. galop.org.uk**

LGBT+ Domestic Abuse Helpline 0800 999 5428

New Pathways "You are not alone. We will believe you. We can support you."

www.newpathways.org.uk 01685 379310

LAY OUT YOUR UNREST ETC

Milton Keynes UK
Ingram Content Group UK Ltd.
UKHW010629160324
439502UK00012B/336